Haunted Hollywood

by Dinah Williams

Consultant: Troy Taylor
President of the American Ghost Society

BEARPORT
PUBLISHING

New York, New York

Credits

Cover and Title Page, © Safet Hadzimusicc/Fotolia, © impulseglamour/iStock, © lunamarina/Fotolia, © woverwolf/Fotolia; 4–5, © Kim Jones; 6, © Helen King/Corbis; 7, © Bruce Torrence; 8, © Courtesy Collection of Donna L. Hill; 9T, © Bettmann/Corbis; 9B, © Courtesy Collection of Donna L. Hill; 10, © picture-alliance/Newscom; 11T, © Axel Koester/Sygma/Corbis; 11B, © Glasshouse Images/Alamy; 12, © John Rice; 13T, © Daily Mail/Rex/Alamy; 13B, © Lee, S. Charles/California State Library; 14, © Wendy Connett/Alamy; 15T, © Pictorial Press Ltd/Alamy; 15B, © Silver Screen Collection/Getty Images; 16, © Tim Lussier/Silents Are Golden; 17, © Bettmann/Corbis/AP Images; 18, © Jon Primrose, theStudioTour.com; 19T, © AF archive/Alamy; 19B, © Moviestore collection Ltd/Alamy; 20, © L.A. Nature Graphics/Shutterstock; 21T, © Wikipedia; 21B, © Conrado/Shutterstock; 22, © Wayne Lorentz/artefaqs.com; 23, © Glasshouse Images/Alamy; 24, © Danger Ranger/Flickr; 25L, © Corbis; 25R, © McManus-Young Collection/Library of Congress/Wikipedia; 26, © LHB Photo/Alamy; 27T, © jondoeforty1/Wikipedia; 27B, © Warner Brothers/Album/Newscom; 31, © Karen Perhus/Shutterstock; 32, © Marina Jay/Shutterstock.

Publisher: Kenn Goin
Creative Director: Spencer Brinker
Design: Dawn Beard Creative
Cover: Kim Jones
Photo Researcher: Picture Perfect Professionals

Library of Congress Cataloging-in-Publication Data

Williams, Dinah (Dinah J.)
  Haunted Hollywood / by Dinah Williams.
    pages cm. — (Scary places–cities)
  Includes bibliographical references and index.
  ISBN 978-1-62724-519-7 (library binding : alk. paper) — ISBN 1-62724-519-7 (library binding : alk. paper)
  1. Ghosts—California—Hollywood—Juvenile literature. 2. Haunted places—California—Hollywood—Juvenile literature. I. Title.
  BF1472.U6W5515 2015
  133.109794'94—dc23

                              2014033298

For more information, write to Bearport Publishing Company, Inc., 45 West 21st Street, Suite 3B, New York, New York 10010. Printed in the United States of America.

10 9 8 7 6 5 4 3 2 1

Contents

As the filmmaking capital of the world, Hollywood has produced lots of scary movies. Ghosts, monsters, and mummies from its studios have made unforgettable on-screen appearances. Yet what if this world-famous spot in southern California is itself haunted by ghosts?

BLACK

BLACK

RETURN OF THE MUMMY

RAVEN

DEATH TAKES A HOLIDAY

In this book you will visit 11 of the spookiest sights in Hollywood and meet many of its most **legendary** ghosts. Among them are an unlucky actress who haunts a well-known landmark, a horror-movie actor who is still seen on his old movie set, and a famed magician who seems to have escaped death. Along the way, you will learn about the history of the "city of dreams," where anyone can become famous—and some try to stay that way forever!

Broken Dreams

The Hollywood Sign

The Hollywood sign is as famous as some of the town's **celebrities**. To many people, it marks a place where dreams come true. Yet for one struggling actress, it was the spot where the hopes of a lifetime ended.

The Hollywood sign

Made up of 45-foot-tall (14 m) letters, the Hollywood sign sits high atop a hill. It was created in 1923 to advertise a community of homes for sale named Hollywoodland. Twenty-six years later, in 1949, city officials dropped the word "land." Now spelling out "Hollywood," the sign reminded all those who saw it of the glitter and promise of the movie industry.

Yet the sign has also been a place of sadness and death. In 1932, a young actress named Peg Entwistle was upset because she could not find work in the movies. On September 16, she left her uncle's small Hollywood home and headed toward the sign. Once there, she climbed a construction ladder and jumped to her death from the top of the letter H.

Since that terrible day, Peg's ghost has been seen haunting the hill, which is now a park. Park rangers and visitors have spotted her in the form of a pretty blond woman in 1930s clothing, most often when it is foggy. Some have also noticed the smell of **gardenias**—the scent found in Peg's favorite perfume.

By 1978, the Hollywood sign was old and worn out. The letters were torn down to make way for a new version made from materials that were stronger and longer lasting. Now, just as before, the letters can be seen for miles.

Peg Entwistle

Refusing to Die

Falcon Lair

Maybe it is because Rudolph Valentino died suddenly at the height of his stardom. Or maybe it is because Valentino strongly believed people could communicate with **spirits**. Whatever the reason, this **silent film** star's ghost has been spotted in many places around Hollywood, including his beautiful Beverly Hills home.

Falcon Lair

In 1925, Rudolph Valentino was an international superstar. To escape his crush of fans, he bought a huge **mansion** behind tall gates in Beverly Hills, an expensive neighborhood near Hollywood. Valentino named the house "Falcon Lair" and filled it with treasures from his many travels. He also had stables for his horses and acres of land for his dogs to run free.

Rudolph Valentino

One short year later, Valentino was dead. Medical problems after surgery for **appendicitis** had killed the 31-year-old actor within days. Thousands of grieving fans attended his funeral.

Not long afterward, Valentino's spirit reportedly began visiting Falcon Lair. His shadowy figure was seen in the halls and staring out the windows. Doors seemed to open and close on their own. One stable worker quit his job after seeing Valentino's spirit petting a horse. There were so many sightings of the movie star's ghost that people who rented the house after his death quickly moved out, convinced it was haunted.

During his life, Valentino believed in the possibility of life beyond the grave and often attended **séances**. Before he died, he wrote in his diary: "What the average man calls Death, I believe to be merely the beginning of Life."

Inside Falcon Lair

The Cemetery Next Door

Paramount Studios

Paramount Studios is a place where many of the world's biggest stars have made films. Right next door is a large cemetery where some of these actors are buried. No wonder the famous studio is now haunted by their ghosts!

Paramount Studios

In the 1920s, Paramount bought 40 acres (16 hectares) from a cemetery called Hollywood Memorial Park to build a new **movie lot**. Soon, the newest part of the giant studio was a busy place, filled with movie crews and actors, including stars such as Bing Crosby, Mae West, the Marx Brothers, and Bob Hope. In time, it would also become filled with ghosts.

Reportedly, most of the ghostly visits occur at night after the movie studio has closed. Guards have repeatedly heard footsteps on the empty stages. They have also seen spirits in old-fashioned clothes. In one of Paramount's oldest structures, the Hart Building, a woman's spirit has been seen on the top floor. She is said to move things around in people's offices, as well as knock them to the floor. The most frightening events, however, have occurred in the area where the studio **borders** the cemetery—some guards say they have seen ghosts passing through a wall there.

Hollywood Memorial Park cemetery

Rudolph Valentino in *The Sheik*

One of Paramount's biggest stars was Rudolph Valentino. When he died unexpectedly in 1926, he was buried next to the studio, in Hollywood Memorial Park. His ghost has since been seen by people in the studio's costume department and by guards. Reportedly, he wears his outfit from *The Sheik*, one of his most famous films.

Movie-Going Ghosts

The Vogue Theatre

In the old days, when people in Hollywood went to the movies, they often went to the Vogue Theatre. For more than 60 years, they lined up there to see films made at nearby studios. Once they got inside, many reportedly saw ghosts as well.

The Vogue Theatre

People say that before the Vogue Theatre was built in downtown Hollywood in 1935, the Prospect Elementary School stood on the same spot. In 1901, a raging fire burned the building to the ground. Twenty-five students were killed, along with their teacher, Miss Elizabeth.

Over the years, many moviegoers inside the Vogue reported seeing the ghosts of children as well as Miss Elizabeth. The spirit of one girl liked to skip up and down the aisle during a movie. She appeared so often that people working at the theater received many complaints.

Later, another ghost began to make appearances. People identify him as Fritz, a movie **projectionist** who worked at the Vogue for nearly 40 years and died of a heart attack in the projection booth. According to some, his spirit would change the film **reels** if the projectionist who was working that day fell asleep on the job.

A movie projectionist

The Vogue Theatre closed in the early 1990s. Today, the building is used for musical performances and other kinds of entertainment. The ghosts from the movie theater have not reappeared—so far.

Inside the Vogue Theatre

13

The Movie Star in the Mirror

Hollywood Roosevelt Hotel

In 1927, the world's biggest film stars attended the opening of the Hollywood Roosevelt Hotel. In the years that followed, many stayed in its beautiful rooms while working on a film or taking a break from filming. Yet it wasn't until 1985, when major work was being done on the building, that some celebrity ghosts came to stay.

The Hollywood Roosevelt Hotel

The Hollywood Roosevelt Hotel is located in the heart of Hollywood. Movie stars have been frequent guests, and one of the most famous was Marilyn Monroe. In the early 1950s, she stayed for months in a room next to the swimming pool.

Marilyn Monroe

During the hotel's **renovation** in the mid-1980s, years after Monroe's death, the mirror from her room was moved to an office downstairs. A hotel maid dusting the mirror saw a beautiful blonde woman reflected in the glass. When she turned around, no one was behind her. Yet the reflection still appeared in the glass. Others have since seen the beautiful movie star reflected there as well.

Another famous ghost haunts Room 928. Actor Montgomery Clift stayed in that room in 1952 while filming a movie. Since his death, his spirit has made itself known to numerous guests. It has appeared by their bed at night, walked the halls with them, and caused the phone to ring nonstop. The haunting is so famous that people now request to stay in the room with Clift's ghost.

The Hollywood Roosevelt Hotel hosted the first **Academy Awards** ceremony in 1929 in its ballroom. Today, many people say there is a mysterious cold spot in the room. Some also say that a man dressed in black haunts the ballroom—though no one knows who he is.

Montgomery Clift

A Ghostly Gathering Place

Pickfair Estate

In 1924, after five years and millions of dollars, the **estate** known as Pickfair was finally finished. The 22-room mansion was the height of **luxury**. It had stables, tennis courts, and the first private in-ground swimming pool in town. Would it also turn out to have ghosts?

Pickfair Estate

Mary Pickford and Douglas Fairbanks were two of the world's most popular film stars when they got married in 1919. Together, they helped start the United Artists film studio. They also built the Pickfair estate, which became the center of Hollywood social life.

While many famous people attended parties at Pickfair, there also seemed to be one uninvited guest. According to some people, the spirit of a woman, dressed as a servant, was seen by Pickford and Fairbanks several times.

After the two stars divorced in 1936, Pickford continued to live in the mansion with her new husband, Buddy Rogers. She stayed until her death in 1979. Then, in 1988, a new couple bought Pickfair and upset many people by tearing down the historic mansion. At the time, they said they did it because of **termite** destruction. However, they later said the real reason was that they were being haunted by a ghost—this time in the form of a mysterious laughing woman.

Some people say that in the months following Mary Pickford's death, Buddy Rogers repeatedly saw her ghost at Pickfair. Each time she appeared, she wore a long white ruffled dress.

Mary Pickford and Douglas Fairbanks at Pickfair

Phantom Stage

Universal Studios

When Universal Studios opened in 1915, the company built and ran the largest movie lot in the world. Today, Universal is still in business, and people flock to the studio tour, hoping to catch a glimpse of their favorite stars. For years, some were lucky enough to see the ghost of a long-ago star as well.

Stage 28 at
Universal Studios

Universal needed a very big lot to film its movies—so big that it could not fit in Hollywood. So the company built its 230-acre (93 hectares) lot a few miles away. With so much space, crews could construct huge sets. One of the most complicated was built on Stage 28 for the 1925 silent film *The **Phantom** of the Opera*. The movie starred Lon Chaney as the Phantom—a mysterious masked figure who haunts the Paris Opera House.

Chaney is truly terrifying as the Phantom. Having grown up with deaf parents, the filmstar learned at a young age how to express himself through acting. He also created his own makeup for the monsterlike face that the Phantom has under his mask. Sadly, only five years after the movie's release, Chaney died.

Lon Chaney as
the Phantom

After his death, the actor was often seen on Stage 28, running around the **catwalks** and wearing the long black cape and mask of his most memorable character. However, the ghostly phantom lost his home when Stage 28 was **demolished** in 2014. Now fans wonder where he will appear next.

Lon Chaney as
the Hunchback

In 1923, Chaney starred in another silent horror movie called *The Hunchback of Notre Dame*. He created his own terrifying makeup for this character, too.

19

Cursed Ground

Griffith Park

Griffith Park is one of the largest and most famous city parks in the world. It has been used as an outdoor location for many film shoots, and it is home to the Hollywood sign. If the stories people tell are true, it is also home to an angry ghost.

Griffith Park

The land that is now Griffith Park was once owned by a wealthy man named Don Antonio Feliz. In 1863, he died suddenly from **smallpox**. According to **legend**, while lying on his deathbed, he was tricked into leaving his property to another wealthy landowner. Furious over losing her **inheritance**, Feliz's 17-year-old niece, Doña Petronilla, put a curse on the land.

Nineteen years later, in 1882, a millionaire named Griffith J. Griffith bought the cursed land. In 1891, he was shot and wounded by a business **rival**. Five years later, he **donated** 3,105 acres (1,256 hectares) to be used as a park—but still could not escape the curse. In 1903, he went to prison for shooting and badly injuring his wife.

Griffith J. Griffith

Several ghosts have been spotted in the park Griffith left behind. The most famous is that of Doña Petronilla. Most often, she haunts the park's trails on horseback, wearing a white dress. She has also been seen on dark, rainy nights in the Paco Feliz Adobe, the oldest structure in the park.

Two other ghostly horseback riders have been reported in Griffith Park as well. One is believed to be Don Antonio Feliz. The other is said to be the spirit of Griffith J. Griffith.

21

The Sound of Spirits

Warner Pacific Theater

To succeed in Hollywood, a person has to work hard. Few have ever worked harder than the Warner brothers. As theater owners and film producers, they were always looking for the next big hit. Some say that one brother, Sam, is still looking.

The Warner
Pacific Theater

By 1924, the four Warner brothers—Harry, Jack, Sam, and Albert—owned the most successful movie studio in Hollywood. The next year, Sam convinced his brothers to take a gamble. In the **era** of the silent film, they decided to create a movie with sound, called *The Jazz Singer*. The brothers also decided to build the gorgeous Warner Pacific Theater to show off this new technology.

Sam worked day and night to make the theater's sound system perfect. Yet on the day before the movie's **premiere** in 1927, he died from **pneumonia**. Some people felt the illness was brought on by stress and working too hard. Whatever the cause, Sam never lived to see *The Jazz Singer* earn millions of dollars, as well as win an Academy Award.

A special sign in Sam's memory was hung in the Warner Pacific Theater in 1928. Soon afterwards, Sam's ghost was seen pacing the lobby. It seems he was not done working. Since then, he has been known to also ride the elevator and move furniture in the upstairs offices.

Sam Warner's ghost has been seen so often that it no longer frightens guards who work in the Warner Pacific Theater.

The Warner brothers—Harry, Jack, Sam, and Albert (left to right)

Escape from Death

Harry Houdini's Home

In 1926, when Harry Houdini died suddenly at age 52, he was one of the most famous men in the world. An escape artist and magician, he amazed audiences by seeming to do the impossible. Was he also able to return from the dead and visit an estate in the Hollywood Hills where he had once lived?

The estate where Houdini lived

Throughout the early 1900s, Harry Houdini thrilled audiences. He escaped from being buried alive, chained up and dunked in water, and suspended high in the air with his arms tightly wrapped. Of course these tricks weren't really brought about by magic. Instead, they were the result of great physical skill and many hours of practice. Yet Houdini actually did believe in the **supernatural**— especially in the possibility of contacting the dead.

During his marriage, Houdini made an agreement with his wife Bess. When one of them died, the two would try to communicate with each other. After Houdini's death, Bess held many séances at an estate overlooking Hollywood. In the 1920s and early 1930s, she and Houdini had lived there.

The séances were never successful, but the famous escape artist may have managed to come back on his own. In 1959, sixteen years after Bess's death, the estate's beautiful main house burned down. Since then, many claim to have seen Houdini's dark figure in its ruins. Often, the ghostly shape has been spotted on a stone staircase in the garden.

Houdini stayed at the estate when he came to Hollywood to make movies. His movies were not nearly as successful as his performances on stage, however, and they did not earn much money.

Harry Houdini

Bess Houdini

Haunted House of Wax

Hollywood Wax Museum

For 50 years, tourists have visited the Hollywood Wax Museum. This unusual attraction—filled with life-size figures of famous stars—is open until midnight 365 days a year. On some dark nights, visitors have seen much more than just their favorite celebrities.

Inside the Hollywood Wax Museum

The Hollywood Wax Museum contains wax figures of hundreds of actors—many of them dressed in the costumes they wore in their best-known movies. As visitors walk through its darkened rooms, they can see Marilyn Monroe, Charlie Chaplin, Angelina Jolie, George Clooney, and other big names from both the past and the present. When they enter a special section called the Horror Chamber, visitors come upon such classic movie monsters as Dracula, Frankenstein, and the Phantom of the Opera.

Not surprisingly, many people find the museum and its lifelike wax figures spooky. Yet there is another reason why being inside the wax museum sends a chill down visitors' spines. When people take photos with the figures at night, something odd is said to happen. Instead of wax figures, strange colored shapes often appear in the photos. A few visitors even claim to have actually seen ghosts moving among the displays.

The Horror Chamber

The Horror Chamber includes a wax figure of actor Vincent Price from the 1953 movie *House of Wax*. In this horror film, he plays the owner of a wax museum who kills people so that he can use their bodies to make life-size figures that will last forever.

Vincent Price in *House of Wax*

27

Universal Studios

A horror-movie actor haunted an old stage set.

Hollywood Wax Museum

Do ghosts lurk among the lifelike wax figures found here?

Falcon Lair

Silent film star Rudolph Valentino still drops by this mansion that he once owned.

Harry Houdini's Home

A famous magician escapes death to appear at his old home.

Hollywood Roosevelt Hotel

Marilyn Monroe and Montgomery Clift are two of the famous guests who have never checked out.

The Vogue Theatre

Audiences saw not just movies, but also ghosts, at this famous theater.

Pickfair Estate

Three ghosts haunt this eerie estate.

BEVERLY HILLS

TO OCEAN

Hollywood Sign

This world-famous landmark is haunted by 1930s actress Peg Entwistle.

Griffith Park

An old curse and an angry spirit haunt this city park.

Warner Pacific Theater

A famous filmmaker is still working hard long after his death.

Paramount Studios

A famed studio is visited by spirits from a cemetery next door.

TO DEATH VALLEY

DOWNTOWN HOLLYWOOD

CANADA

Hollywood, CA   UNITED STATES
OF AMERICA

MEXICO

Glossary

Academy Awards (uh-KAD-uh-mee uh-WARDZ) important awards given every year to actors, directors, and others in the movie industry

appendicitis (uh-*pen*-duh-SYE-tiss) a dangerous illness in which an organ in the body called the appendix is infected by germs

borders (BOR-durz) meets along a common line or edge

catwalks (KAT-wawks) narrow walkways

celebrities (suh-LEB-ruh-teez) very famous people

demolished (di-MOL-ishd) torn down

donated (DOH-nayt-id) gave as a gift

era (IHR-uh) time period

estate (ess-TAYT) a large property, including land, a house, and sometimes other buildings

gardenias (gar-DEEN-yuhs) white flowers with a strong, sweet smell

inheritance (in-HER-uh-tuhnss) property received from someone upon that person's death

legend (LEJ-uhnd) a story from the past that is not always completely true

legendary (LEJ-uhn-*der*-ee) very famous

luxury (LUHK-shuh-ree) something expensive and beautiful that makes life enjoyable and pleasant

mansion (MAN-shuhn) a very large house

movie lot (MOO-vee LOT) an outdoor area in which buildings or scenery are put up so that scenes from movies can be filmed

phantom (FAN-tuhm) a ghost or spirit

pneumonia (noo-MOH-nyuh) a disease of the lungs that makes it difficult to breathe

premiere (pruh-MYAIR) the first showing of a movie or other entertainment event

projectionist (pruh-JEK-shuhn-ist) a person who operates the machines that show films in a theater

reels (REELZ) spools

renovation (*ren*-uh-VAY-shuhn) work done to improve the condition of something

rival (RYE-vuhl) someone who is competing against another person

séances (SAY-ahnss-iz) meetings at which people attempt to make contact with the dead

silent film (SYE-luhnt FILM) a movie in which there is no recorded sound

smallpox (SMAWL-*poks*) a disease that causes high fever and is often deadly

spirits (SPIHR-its) otherworldly creatures, such as ghosts

supernatural (*soo*-pur-NACH-ur-uhl) something unusual that breaks the laws of nature

termite (TUR-mite) an insect that looks like an ant and eats wood

Bibliography

Jacobson, Laurie. *Hollywood Haunted.* Santa Monica, CA: Angel City Press (1999).

Ogden, Tom. *Haunted Hollywood.* Guilford, CT: Globe Pequot (2009).

Parish, James. *The Hollywood Book of Death.* Columbus, OH: McGraw-Hill (2001).

Read More

Horak, Jan-Christopher, et al. *Hooray for Hollywood and the Rise of Motion Pictures.* Peterborough, NH: Cobblestone Publishing (2007).

Lunis, Natalie. *A Haunted Capital (Scary Places: Cities).* New York: Bearport (2015).

Schnobrich, Emily. *California: The Golden State (Exploring the States Blastoff! Readers).* Minneapolis, MN: Bellwether (2013).

Learn More Online

To learn more about haunted Hollywood, visit
www.bearportpublishing.com/ScaryPlaces

Index

About the Author

Dinah Williams is an editor and children's book author. Her books include *Abandoned Amusement Parks; Haunted Prisons; Monstrous Morgues of the Past;* and *Spooky Cemeteries*, which won the Children's Choice Award. She lives in Cranford, New Jersey.